Ephemeral Moments

A collection of poetry and short stories

Ayvaunn Penn

First Edition: June 2013

Volume 1

The characters and events portrayed in this book are all inspired by true events.
Names of people, places, and things have been changed to protect identities. Any
similarities to real persons (living or dead), places, or things are coincidental and
not intended by the author. Views expressed in this book do not reflect those of
Your Black Poets or any of its affiliate websites.

ISBN-13: 978-0615747903 (Ayvaunn Penn, In(k))

DEDICATION

To the mission of fulfilling the calling God has on my life to use the lyrical and prosaic gift in witness of His mercy, glory, and greatness. To all who are human yet perplexed by the human condition. To all those conscious of their immortal spirit while simultaneously celebrating the ephemerality of mortal moments.

CONTENTS

Poetry

Short Stories

ACKNOWLEDGMENTS

First giving honor to my Lord and Savior Jesus Christ, I would like to thank my mother and father for the invaluable gifts of life, love, and support. To all those whose lives have touched mine and served as inspiration, thank you. To Dr. Roger Platizky I offer gratitude for not only recognizing, nurturing, and believing in the writer he saw in me – especially the poet – but for also making me believe in her, too. Finally, thanks to Norman Silver and his company, Spectra Studios, for the wonderful photography.

AUTHOR'S NOTE

Dear Readers:

Although this book is comprised of poetry and prose and the following is applicable to both, I would like to especially address the first. Poetry is about capturing, conveying, and celebrating the raw emotions felt by one in an instant. To censor genuine pain, joy, or anger is to lie, and that is farthest from my objective. Here, you will find the up-close, the real, the personal, the gut-wrenching, the good, and the bad. Here, you will find the perplexities of humanity. Perhaps, you will even find yourself. As a called writer, it is my duty to unfurl what others rather keep hidden. Vulnerable human to vulnerable human, you are being invited into the deepest darkest crevices of the mind – a place that most choose to hide. Let us sup from the cup of humanity together. Welcome.

Affectionately,
Ayvaunn Penn
ayvaunnpenn@gmail.com

" ³Blessed be God, even the Father of our Lord Jesus Christ, the Father of mercies, and the God of all comfort; ⁴Who comforteth us in all our tribulation, that we may be able to comfort them which are in any trouble, by the comfort wherewith we ourselves are comforted of God."

II Corinthians 1: 3 – 4

Poetry

Ephemeral Moments

EPHEMERAL MOMENT

In a split second of my ephemeral moment in time
I blinked
And without warning
My world collapsed into an unbelievable greatness
Of just me
And God

And
In that moment
Of sometime
In the latter months
Of 2010
Without warning
I felt
It

It was me who said "It's okay"
It was me who had no worries
It was me who passed the days care free
But not today
Today, without warning
I felt
It

And all of a sudden
It
Was out of my control
As I gazed out of the glass
My eyes turned to glass
Before I knew
It
I felt the burn and my own independence crept up on me
Slapped me in the face and said
"I'm here"
And in that instant I felt the fear
The uncertainty
And
This tear split the second

When Aloneness stabbed me in my side

Out poured tears
Not mine, but those my mother had cried
And why?
Why was it that for this moment I, I was not okay?

It was the same day my father sold my memories away
It was the day I realized my own homelessness
And for that split second of my ephemeral moment in time
I
I was not okay

THE TRUTH ABOUT TRUTH

Tell me when the truth ain't ugly
Tell me when the truth don't hurt
Somebody
Please tell me
When's Truth gonna' do as she promised?
When is Truth going to set   me   free?

The truth is
I'm tired of this hell hole engulfing me
The truth is that this hurts
Somebody
Please tell me
What ever possessed me to put you first?
What ever possessed me to endure the worst?

Tell me when your love was ever patient
Tell me when your love was ever kind
Somebody
Please tell me
Why, instead, your love made me a patient, and
Why, instead, your love left me blind

The truth is
I never should have called you mine
The truth is
I was never yours
The truth is
We were NEVER meant to be
The sound of that ain't so ugly, and
Of that I am sure
In fact, it sounds quite beautiful indeed

You see, had I listened to Truth
You wouldn't have had the chance to hurt me
I never would have put you first, and
I never would have endured the worst
I would have waited for love with patience, and
I would have found one who was kind
    One who most certainly would not have left me blind

So…
I can tell you when the truth ain't ugly
I can tell ya' when the truth don't hurt
I can tell ya' Truth will free you as she promised
But, only if you heed her words
And, baby, that's the truth about Truth
The only time she ever hurts
Is when you fail to listen
To her
First

BACK-HAND

They all tell me
I look just like you
But, where are you?
You were never anywhere to be found
No fair.
How dare you deny Me
Without giving me the chance to deny You

You took everything we had
And spent it on yourself.
Yeah, you could argue
You didn't leave us in the cold
Yeah, you could argue
That you put food on the table
You could even say
That you put clothes on my back

But what about
That back-hand slap?
What about
The way you not only cursed out Mama
But cursed ya' scared toddlin' babe too?
What about the nights I awoke
To Mama's heavin' cry?
Tell me why
When you and Mama were arguin'
I was so sick of the yellin'
The shattered glass
The threats
So sick, I literally vomited

Ok.
So you were there for
That
Personally...
I ain't heard'a no lil' girl who wanted
That
That ain't what I call bein' there.

But you know what?

Imma' make a deal with you
Say you were there.
Just, take ya' last name back
Say you were there
And I promise you
I'll pray my kids don't look a thing like You
Say you were there
And we can be through
I
Deny
You

THE LIST THAT CEASES FIRE

From a very early age
4 to be exact
I already had a list of all the things I knew
I wouldn't put my children through

Somewhere around number one on that list was this
"Don't argue in front of my children"
Well let me tell you
I'm 21 and 5 months away from 22
Sitting in my room
Listening to my parents do what they've always done
And it appears they will never cease to do

Argue

To be completely honest I thought by now I'd be fully immune
Apparently not
'Cause they're interrupting my thought process on this paper I have due
Daddy's rage
Mama's yell
Even now when I hear his voice hit a certain range
I still get afraid

Well...
They been married what? 18 years?
Oh, 28
Look at me
I made a specific point of not counting
Because I declare it's a miracle I'm here
A wonder I didn't drown in my infinite tears
All accumulated in my meager years

And...
You mean to tell me your voices aren't tired
Are you, too, not sick of the constant ire?
Perhaps not
'Cause even today my grown-woman tears were not too tired
To prick my eyes with a burning something like fire

I don't give a…
If your voices never in my lifetime retire
Here's the 1 thing I desire
Imma' keep my list
And hold true to it
I'll have you know
The eyes of my children will never have to burn from fire
     of a love that was never true
As my eyes, at your hands, so often do

Perhaps
Just for laughs
I'll even given them the list as an heirloom
And 1 day while they're sitting on your lap
Eyes strikingly aglow
You'll wonder why
Well, from my kids to you
I say
"Thank you"

A FAMILIAR IGNORANCE

You there
The kin
With my blood
Hold your tongue
As I ask the Good Lord to help me forgive you
For you know and know not what you do

You babble behind backs
Speaking of me as slack
As if you really know about that
Shut up your ignorance.
You may only speak when you've walked in my tracks

You say I should help the man
    Get a job
I will when you tell me what you know of my midnight sobs
You say I should help my husband
    Get out of this financial mess
I will when you tell me what you know of my marriage's ugliness
You say I am wrong for reservation of assistance
I will never say I am wrong, but
I will let you tell me what you know
Of how he beat me so

The truth is
You
Don't
Know
'Cause you always told me, "Hush, baby. The world don't need to know."
Well now I'm tellin' you to hush
'Cause when I tried to tell you how badly he was treating me
You didn't want to hear it
Something about that seems laughable to me

Women of my kin
How could YOU of all people say such things?
The same women who have suffered at the hands of their own men for
    greater things
You would curse me for removing my wedding ring
That is only because my story is akin to the one your heart sings

And whereas I have loosed Myself
You long to be free

So, Father, help me forgive them, for they know what they do
Free them from the chains of abuse
This, Lord, I pray of You

TREAT ME BAD SO I CAN WRITE ABOUT IT

Go on ahead and treat me bad
So I can write about it
Falsely accuse me
Imma' tell the world about it

I welcome filthy words you spit so bold
Little do you know they're dusted in gold
Dilapidated words you draw from hell's well
Liquidate your assets and make them my wealth
Speak on, dim wit
You only fortify my health
How can that be?
Stop asking dumb questions
You oughta' know the Good Lord ain't gon' let you break me

Go on ahead and utter hate in my face
Fill this place with your ugly words of hate
Go on ahead and call me out of my name
Every word you speak puts food on my plate
Try with all your might to tear me down and
smear upon my face a despairing frown

I see you laughing there
I see
You think I'm insane
You must have forgotten
I can call on my Jesus' name

He's taught me not to despair
And I shol'nuf don't frown
Oh, but you done done it now
You done put yo' hands on His child
Best believe He don't take kindly to that
There ain't no need for me to take a knife to yo' back
I repeat
There ain't no need for me to get back
Cause, baby, I know MY God's covered that

The good Lord told me not to call a man a fool
So… look'a'here
Be ye wise
Heed the words I say
If I were, you, I'd be afraid

God is just getting started with you
Very honestly I don't know what He's gon' do
Despair may have to teach your heart new tricks
Frowns may contort your face in weird twists
I don't know what the Lord's gon' do
But this I do know

You might as well pack up you and all yo' mess
'Cause, baby, I'm through
I ain't worried
'Cause God's got you

PRAY, BELIEVE, AND BE HEALED

Pray
Believe
And you'll be healed
That's what the Believers keep telling me
Well let me tell ya'
I been prayin'
And believin'
And over this month and a half
I
Have not
Been
Healed

I can hear it now
"She don't really believe.
She woulda' been cured by now."
I can hear it now
"What have you done that the Lord won't make you whole?"
I can hear it now
"And she calls herself a Christian. Where's her Lord?
What kind of fool follows a fickle God?"
I can hear it now
…myself asking
"God, why?"

I ain't gon' lie
Many tears have I cried
On the note of not lying…
I still cry
Since the first day this illness hit
I've poured over the healing scripts
Reading in the book of Matthew
How my good Lord healed
Leprosy
Palsy
And praying and proclaiming with all of my being
I just knew He would heal me
And on this 14th day of the 10th month of 2011
My flesh is still afflicted
This is my human reality

So this human being began to question God
And this human asked:

Why me?
The girl with faith brimming
The girl who looks to You everything
The girl who acknowledges that without You she is nothing
Why me?
The girl who inquired of You her purpose so diligently
The girl who lends her ear to You so earnestly
The girl who finally came to be at peace with that discovery
The girl who You called to write "Why me?"

God, I have prayed
God, I have believed
God, I am waiting
Do you hear me?
Does my faith mean nothing to you?
Why have you not healed me?
My flesh whispers that you mock me
Why are you taking so long?

Into my spirit did my Jesus whisper this song
A sweet melody of reminders of His love
A kind chastisement of my doubt to draw me back into His arms
Reeling me in before my mind was too far gone
These thoughts the Lord brought to me:

God will heal me
I'm on God's time
Not my own
Besides
All things are for His glory
Not my own
God would not be God if I could command Him to do as I say
    When I say
I may call upon God and trust in God to keep the promises He made
But I should not be dismayed or think He has failed me
Just because He does not do what I want
When I want
This is a trying of my faith to make me stronger

Then all was still
And to me did God draw near
It was as though a hand drew back my hair
And a strong voice whispered tenderly in my ear:

> Doubt no longer
> My Word declares that it is already done
> Your prayers and belief are not for none
> Doubt ye no longer
> Your time does mine exceed
> Patience, Merrily
> You are healed
> When your time meets mine
> Not only will you see, but
> Feel

SLAIN GALL

Stop!
I command you
Let me go
You can bind me no more
From this day forward
I declare Freedom
Never again
Will your chains chafe me

Soar

Yes, that I will.
Watch me fly
I rise, a Woman

Strong

You must not have known
What you were stomping to the ground
That expression says it all

Haha

What gall
To think
You could hold me down
Shatter my Will
No
You could not have known

I am telling you
Gone is the day of broken

Will

Has conjured the pieces of me

s   c   a   t   t   e   r   e   d

I am not
I am

Whole

I
Hold
My
Own
My own roots
I water
The good Lord is my sun
With Him I spring forth
Full bloom
Triumphant
Sturdy stalk
Blushing
Golden
Petals
Tan face forever turning towards the Son
Every morning shedding dewy tears
That kiss the ground from which I sprung
Thankful to the Son
For bathing me in the rays of His love

t   r   a   m   p   l   e   d

I am not
I stand

Tall

I JUST SAW TWO HAWKS SOAR BY...

Preface

I was studying for finals in the library. I had a window seat. Or should I say, I had window seats. Two cushy purple chairs had I pulled together — one for my romp and one for my feet. The view was so lovely that for a few moments I could not start my work but only gaze out of the glass. And in that momentous span, I looked up just in time to catch two black hawks soar from midway the window frame, to the corner, beyond the reach of my sight but not yet out of my mind. Of all mothers, you — Nature, are the only one who has no problems diverting my attention from my studies. However, I do not believe I could call shame upon you.

~

I just saw two hawks soar by
So high
So graceful
For a moment
I was caught up in the same current as they
Before I knew it
We were all three whisked away

I AM A MORGUE

I am a morgue
In this filthy world in which I live
My lungs expand with death
The food that nourishes me is poison running through my veins
I am walking mortality
You too
We are all dead
Don't believe this is only me
It's you, too, you ought to see
You should be able to see, feel, and taste that we are all dead

Cars carelessly, relentlessly sneeze their germs into the air
The wind wheezes and coughs up smog
The food is ill
It suffers from pesticides and human-induced genetic mutation
Right
What God made good
The air is so sick that even the moss refuses grow

We, the living dead, have committed this
We, the perpetrating dead, must pray for forgiveness
We, the dead, must fix it

11:01PM, UGH, VALENTINE'S DAY

The rise of secret admirers
The fall of that tide
Ugh
It would subside
On the day
Of love

It's just another day
So why turn away
From the one
You know
You're
Crushing
On

Yeah
I heard
They told me
I was blind
Why is the crush-ee always the last one to know?

I vomited today
Not in lament of you
My body bled
But not
For either of you

You know
It woulda' been nice
Had you sent a text
Yeah
Like the "Good Morning" you sent just yesterday
Remember
It's just another day
But all the same
It woulda' been nice
Seeing as on this just-another-day
Of love
I was sick
It woulda' been nice

So
There went the tide
The rise, the fall of infatuated love
The day before
They're all over you
The day of
They avoid you
Come the day after
I dare you
I dare you to approach me
Why couldn't you do that for me today?
The day I coulda' actually used that text
Today, this just-another-day
Ugh
Happy Valentine 's Day to
You, too
Love

TONIGHT, WE TALK

My tongue is bold
I always said my words would change the world, and it starts
Right
Here

Draw ye near
No?
Well my words will pull you by your ear
And your flesh may get seared
But, the truth hurts

There's something going on here
Hush, don't talk about it
But, there's talk among my peers
My beautifully black peers
We talk amongst ourselves, but hush
We keep it hushed
There is fear of speaking in the presence of your ear

But, tonight, we talk

Taste it
Feel it on the regions of your tongue
What was often sweetly hidden is now turned bitter
Too tart to speak of
But tonight we bite the lemon, hard
Tonight we'll savor the tart truth
Tonight we will all share in the constant burn of the black student's plight

Tonight, we talk

It would be a shame for us to come to this diverse place and leave
        unchanged
It's a sad thing that some leave culturally maimed
Yes, it happens here

But, tonight, we talk

We all come from different walks of life
Some of us, more than others, have had to deal with strife
But whatever you have had to deal with in your life
Know that when you come here
You should learn to walk many different walks of life
And if you have not already?

That is why, tonight, we talk

This is what we boast – a diverse student body population
We would also like to think we can boast harmony
Not racial trials and tribulations
Let us take a moment to check ourselves

As tonight, we talk

A dedicated SDB member, I've had visiting parents ask me if I feel accepted
I always say yes, for largely, this is the case
But largely philosophically means that there is no doubt a "smally"
In a smaller yet sufficient percent of the time
Black students do not feel welcome here
We know because we tell each other

But, tonight, I talk

Black
Some people still don't know what to do with it
Some say it's overrated and just want to be through with it
Race
Some say we need to get over ourselves
They think we're past this
Yes, our nation has made progress
But, we?
We are not through with this

And that's why, tonight, we talk

Yes, that is the truth you hear
What is the truth of what goes on here?
Well, let me grace your ears

Look at black like it belongs here
Black also deserves to be lent your ear
Don't fear sitting down to eat with a group of us
Don't fear approaching a throng of us
When you're working on a project with me, don't you dare overlook my
     intelligence
Don't you forget I sit right alongside YOU in OUR classes
Don't be afraid to participate in Black Expressions
People of all races participate in Los Amigos, MSA, ASA, and ICA
Please know that B.E. is just the same

Please don't be amazed when I succeed just as well as you do
Please don't be floored if I surpass you

This isn't in our heads
It's the truth and everyone knows it
Oh, yes, you can choose to hide it
You can deny it
But you CAN see it
It's just that too often we close our eyes to it
Hush
But, it's time for that to stop

And don't get mad at me when I speak the truth
Don't brush me off
If you want to know when we'll stop
This is when we'll stop
When you look at us like we belong here

Well whatever is she talking about?

Just for a moment
I require you
Step into the life of a black student
Listen to the truth of goings on here:
     "An RA said, 'It would be the black people on the hall making all of
     that noise.'"
     "An Asian student said, 'But wouldn't it be weird for me to be sitting
     at a table with just black people?'"
     A white student in a philosophy course made an outrageous comment
     concerning African Americans. The entire class gasped, stared down
     the lone black student and awaited a reaction. Another white student
     dropped and shook his head muttering, 'That was so unnecessary.'

Now, I make you privy to the lamentations of black students that often
    escape your ears
Listen:
> "I have to try so hard every day not to get worked up about it. I've
> tried talking to my roommate, but she isn't trying to hear me. She'll
> never know what it's like to be black. She'll never know what it's like
> to be me."
> "I notice the small things. How they'll hold the door open for them,
> but let the door slam in my face."
> "The way they look at me when I say I'm pre-med. Like I just spoke in
> gibberish or something."
> "If you're Asian, you're expected to be smart, if you're white, you can
> be smart, if you're black, you have to prove it first."
> "When I show up to class, this same kid always turns rap music on his
> iPod, and greets me like 'yo, wassup?'"
> "In sociology class, everyone has something to say every day until we
> get to the race and ethnicity unit covering books like *Why Do All the
> Black Kids Sit Together in the Cafeteria?*. Then everyone is silent. Some get
> offended by their own choice ignorance."

Open up your eyes
This many people wouldn't be lyin' for the hell of it
It may not be YOU discriminating, but
Yes, today the issue is still relevant

That's why, tonight, we talked

These bitter truths don't reflect everybody, I know
If it's not you, thank you, and make sure it's never you
But if today you looked yourself in the mirror of my words
You've got to change because the beginning of the end of this
Is today

~

Terms and Acronyms
    SDB: Student Development Board, a college organization comprised of students
who help out with major campus events often involving but not limited to
prospective students and their families
    Black Expressions (B.E.): a college student organization with the mission of
raising awareness about African-American culture on campus and in the local
community
    Los Amigos: a college student organization with the mission of raising awareness
about Hispanic culture on campus and in the local community
    MSA: Muslim Student Association, a college organization with the mission of
raising awareness about Muslim culture on campus and in the local community

ASA: Asian Student Association, a college student organization with the mission of raising awareness about Asian culture on campus and in the local community
ICA: Indian Cultural Association, a college student organization with the mission of raising awareness about Indian culture on campus and in the local community
RA: Resident Assistant, students who assist in managing dormitories

BLACK IS JUST AS RIGHT

Lies
Everything white ain't right
Yet, we've been taught to believe that it is
It is time for that to come to an end
I shall believe in that lie never again
Today I chant a new anthem

How many of you know that everything black is right
No, Jesus is not white
How many of you are familiar with the black man's plight
    And know all too well about the white flight
      How all through history they tried to fly far from our
      sight
Oh, but black people, too, can take flight
    Watch us soar
    Watch us fly
    Watch us fly deep into the midnight sky
And know, we're not coming back
For we refuse to ever re-track
Always taking fresh steps into the future
Higher and higher with every living breath
And know, no, no
We never waste time to look back

Why?
It's not because black is the new white
It's because Black is just as Right

Lies
Everything white ain't right
Yes, we've been taught to believe it is
But that day has come to an end
I'll never believe that lie again
Because this is my new anthem

LES LEÇONS DE L'AMOUR

How many people can write about love?
How many people can write about differences?
How many people can write about those unfortunate instances
  When the one they love
  Is sitting right next to them
  Yet simultaneously
  At an unfathomable distance?
How many people can write about mistakes?
How many people can write about being misled?
How many people can admit
  They never should have engaged in something
  They didn't see fully feasible in their head?
How many people felt they were right?
How many people will admit they were wrong?
How many people will open their eyes to see
  Neither of the latter two truly have a voice
  It's Reality that resounds loud and strong

PATHETIC FALLACY

Snip snip!
There was never a sound so sweet
To that strong, bold, robust tree striving towards its peak
As the pruning back of dead branches, and
The trimming of dead leaves
We all have roots, and
We all have trunks
Don't let impeding things and people in your life
Keep you
Stumped

Best believe
That tree is me
Best believe
You are more than a dead leaf to me
You're a big ole burdensome branch, and
I don't know how for
    So long
I let that be

In the fall we fell for each other
In the winter we were close
When April showers should have nurtured our love
We were ready to spring away from each other

The Bible tells me there's a time and season for everything
Now it's spring
April showers have borne May flowers
Including the ones on weeds
And now it's time to clean

In my garden you were once a flower
Now I count you a weed
I need not question the transformation
But only recall your thistly deeds
If you did sow a little more good than bad
Don't forget hairy seeds do thistles breed
And when April showers away the fall
She cannot help but foster the garden
All

Big ole burdensome branch
Prickly weed with a blossom and all
Snip snip!
There was never a sound so sweet
As the pruning back of dead branches
The uprooting of weeds, and
The flourishing of me

…IT HAPPENS

Good times with the wrong person
    …it happens
Fond memories with the person you're not so fond of
    …it happens
Wondering how you ever thought you could be with that person
    …it happens
Wanting desperately to forget but not being able for the life of you to forget
    …it happens

Wondering why you can't shake him
Knowing she did you wrong but you just can't shake her
You know you don't want him
You know you don't love her
Got you racking out your brain wondering why on earth
    … it happens

I'm not your other exes that you swear to this day want you back
And that's a fact
What's that you used to say?
"Don't get it twisted."
You ain't no good
I'll NEVER want you back

So why is it that
At the most random moments I laugh
Thinking about our good times
    I don't want that to happen

And why is it that
Out of all your hell
I can recall even one fond moment to tell
    I'd give anything for that not to happen

And forget me wondering NOW how I ever could have been with you
I had to do too much questioning in the midst of our relationship too
    That should NEVER happen

But all I can resolve is that, sometimes
    …it happens

COLLEGE HABIT

Preface
Senior year. It's the week before my next-to-last round of college finals, and I'm in the library trying to get focused. My objective at the moment is to start writing my 20 page paper that is due in rough draft on Thursday. The bad thing is that today is Tuesday. Anyhow, my mind is drifting, and opposed to the words for my paper coming to mind, this came to me instead.

~

Comfy in a chair
Laptop on my knees
Staring at blank page
A 20 page paper is calling my name

In the corner there is a gleam
A crisp image of the scene behind me
Behold
No other place than on my computer screen

Though within library doors
My eyes sense a breeze
God must have exhaled
There moves each leaf of each tree

In such regal air
No thing of nature can despair
All robed in autumnal brown
Each not-so-evergreen bough does bow

My head is about to do the same
But, not in Jesus' name
In case you couldn't guess...
I'm tired

Attention! Reel in from nature's radiance
I focus once again upon GPA maintenance

CRYING INTO PANTIES

Cappuccino legs crossed neatly
amid laundry littering
the top
of an unruly bed

Tan legs
Fresh laundry
Hot tears falling
Frantic hands fumbling
Fingers grasping
Pressing
A pair
Of black cotton underwear
To her face of despair

~

Sitting cross legged and crying into a pair of black cotton underwear
I would let my shirt sop my let-loose tears, but... I still have makeup on
Don't want to stain it
My MAC NC45 tainted tears would be traceless on the undies, though
Invisible, lost in a world of possibly numerable threads
Feeling particularly alone
Much like myself
Rather alone
Especially alone
Trying to figure out the other feelins I'm feelin'
Have you ever been there?
When you don't even know why you're cryin'
I mean, I'm not even close to my period
So I shouldn't even be this emotional
And man I'm thinkin'
Must have really hit an all-time low to cry into panties
PANTIES
They're clean and all, but still
What is this I feel?
Why is it that my humors began to spill from my eyes as I made myself
    Proclaim out loud what I heard the preacher say?
"Thank you, God, for the closed doors as much as the open ones."
And then my tear ducts just couldn't behave anymore
What is this I'm feeling?

I feel so lost like I'm floundering
Can't breathe like I'm drowning
I'm not used to this
Not having direction
This staying-still business
I know the good Lord told me to wait patiently, and I'm trying
What is this not-quite tension doing in my chest?
Why do I feel like I'm consumed in madness?
Could scream, laugh, cry all at the same time
One down, two to go, right?
I don't even know what to do with myself anymore
How many jobs can I apply for?
How many slammed shut doors without even telling me?
All except one company
They took such careful time to write me saying
"We are unable to match your qualifications at this time,
But we would like to thank you for taking the time to explore our career
Opportunities."
I almost wish they were like the others
And didn't bother to give me the common courtesy
Why is my body doing strange things?
Needles running through my pelvis
Flares of acne, and
My hair is shedding profusely
And my ex
My EX
Don't get me started on my ex
He's not even worth my breath, but
I can't manage to get him out my head
And the 'rents
The 'rents
When?! Tell me when will they get a divorce already?
It's been a long time coming
Neither of them are happy
They're not doing anyone any favors
No, not them
No, not even me
Please just sign the papers, and
Me
God, I'm interested to know how You're using this portion of my life as
        Training
God, I don' t like it
No one can hide anything from You

41

This doesn't feel good to me
I'd be in trouble if I needed more than a mustard seed
Lord, my heart knows that You've got this,
That THIS…is all a part of your plan to mold me and make me
This, Lord, I pray, but
My mortal mind is having a tough time wrestling with this
All of this uncertainty
What is this I'm feeling?
Sitting cross-legged amongst my laundry
Crying tears
Into panties

~

My tan legs
My fresh laundry
My hot tears falling
My frantic hands fumbling
Fingers grasping
Pressing
A pair
Of black cotton underwear
To my face of despair

QUEL AGE SOMMES NOUS?

You're going to let that stop you?
What is age?
You know, I used to feel the same way
It was a sin to be older than a man
One you were considering to be your companion
Absolutely abominable
Until one day Austin came along
I never thought twice about him
We kind of grew up together
Both aware of the other one's presence in the same church
But apparently he was a tad bit more aware of me
Than at that time I believed
Time passed
Our days, Time spent
Off to college we both went
But in different directions, Time rent
Only to cross our threads
Bringing us nigh each other once again
And God bless that social network dubbed Facebook
That's how he found me
And but of course, we started talking
We exchanged numbers
And he began to text me "Good morning"
And before I knew it
He was expressing his interest in me
And that's when it hit me
"He's younger than me."
But I looked back at our chatting
I looked back at our history
And I realized "This is a good guy.
It'd be silly not to give him a try
All behind a number called age."
It was a pleasant experience
Austin and I
But as Time spent our days
She rent our threads
And, once again, began sowing our lives separate ways
No malice or hate
No rhyme or reason
Or perhaps, it just was not our season

But now here we are
You and I
This is the second time you have expressed interest in me
Expressed that you have favor with me
Expressed that you don't at all mind the idea of being with me
It is also the second time you have taken it back
And now you are saying
"I have prayed to the Lord about it
Spoken to the Lord specifically 'bout it
I have come to the decision that we should just remain friends."
What is age?
Do you not know that wisdom has been known to pour from the mouth of
     babes?
Surely you know that even the elders do foolish things?
What is age?
Nothing
The mind is timeless
The soul – immortal
Those are what compose a person
Those are the measures by which you check your compatibility with
     another
That is why a significant other is called a soul-mate
Not the number of days they walked on the earth
Not how fresh or worn the brow
Or else a significant other would be called an age-mate
And you said you prayed about it?
And the fact that you're a year younger than me was the determining factor?
You mean to tell me you prayed to God about a number?
You think God has a mate set aside for you based mainly on a number?
Ok
I can't judge your relationship with God
Or change your mind about anything
If you want to be friends based on a number
Fine, your loss
Just know we will only ever be friends
We'll never go down that road again
But because I am first and foremost your friend
Allow me to save your rear end
And protect you from ruining your chances with another good-potential
     girlfriend
Repeat after me:
"What is age? Nothing."

THORN IN MY SIDE

Gladly did I lay down me
Upon the sands so humbly
To the Lord my side did I reveal
Closed my eyes
And was still

I rested in the Lord and was at peace
Rest did I in the Lord
But flesh against my spirit in me did war
Quickly did my Lord cease the fire
Lest more against my spirit my flesh could conspire

When I was done resting in the Lord
I opened my eyes
And beheld in my side
This thorn

~

This thorn do not I hide
I boast to call it mine
Not only of God's existence does it constantly remind me,
But that no matter how great my success is
    It is always because of Him, never because of me
It reminds me of my place,
That the Lord's not behind me
    That God is God
    Not me

Though for some it would drive them insane
This thorn in my side is nothing near my existence's bane

For Moses it was a stutter
For me it's a muscle mutter
For you some vice of some other
And when the eyes of others fall upon it
Dare ye not to hide it
But yours boast to call it
For some thorn of some form God all of us adorns

So it was gladly that I laid down my pride
And with closed eyes
Trusted the Lord to pierce me

Inspired by
II Corinthians 12:7 – 10

MY FIRST COUNTRY WEDDING

No veil
No train
Not even a white gown
But a crown?

Folding chairs
Monkey grass
Horse flies
Stemmed glass?

Sticky heat
Pitched tent
Two rings
Popsicle maid?

"I do"

Deep South
Deep country
Deep passion
Deep love

TRUE POETRY

No
One cannot simply sit down and say
"Today I write poetry."
It blossoms into being when moved to smiles or frowns
Then as the conceived poem in your head rattles 'round
It sends you frantically for a pen, so
You can jot your thoughts down
You see, my friends
True poetry is born out of the passions
  The imbalance of the humors John Milton's predecessors spoke of so
  Seriously
None of this "ode to the flower" this
Or "ode to the rock" that
I hate to break it to you, but
If the author was not inspired by that flower
Or that rock
That author's poem is smack
In fact, it ain't even a poem to be exact
Now many a great poet has written about the flower
Many a great poet has written about the rock
What made them great was not merely that they were inspired
It was not merely the thought
Gosh darn it!
Tell me who ain't great that can make me revere a flower as regal
Or even think twice about a rock
The prodding of the humors
The evoking of the emotions
The excitement of the passions
That's what poetry is made of
If it don't strike a chord in you or me
Quite frankly, it ain't worthy of the title
Poetry

I JUST WANT TO WRITE

Let me tell you what it takes to be a phenomenal writer
What does it take to be a phenomenal writer?
To stand above all others
Aspiring
Wishing
To be that same great thing?
  And you must know that a writer
  IS
  A great thing
It takes courage
Many people utter their words into the air
But not all are fearless enough to etch their thoughts into permanent form
To be beheld for all eternity
We'd like to think a man's thoughts are his own
That they dwell in the cranial abode awaiting release
No
Words' persons are their own
Yes
Words' persons are their own
They prowl the earth seeking whom they may indwell
They don't just seek anyone
Words want one of those
  Great things
  A writer
These beings
These things that convey meaning desire to be had
By one who will keep their timelessness
Timeless
So
It is not merely my yearning
"I just want to write."
Words have procured the bold willing me
I am chosen to write
And I answer the call

WAITING FOR MY HERSHEY'S KISS

Chocolate
You enrapture me
Brimming with passion strong and dark
Seed of cacao, melt on my tongue
Leave me wide-eyed and drunken
I cannot resist your delight
I yearn for your boldness
Grip me by my senses
Tight

Vanilla
You tease me
You, too, are sweet
Delicate is your touch
You leave me with no complaint
Chaud ou froid, you are always decent pleasure
But this, my senses wonder:
Will you ever measure up to the cocoa of the tree?
Could you ever hit the spot?

~ Ayvaunn Penn

~

I'd always wanted me a Black man: educated, good job, clean cut, filled with the Holy Ghost and the finest of God's good work. Growing up, I went through ten years of private school. Aside from church once a week I didn't see much of the brothas. Because the fact of the matter is, not many African-American families pay extra big bucks for their kids to attend private school. So it was. For the longest time, I was the only Black girl in my classes along with two other Black boys. I wasn't worried about the boys during elementary. They were gross. Yet just like any youngin', my hormones went a'churnin' when middle school came along. Don't get me wrong. I wasn't what you'd call boy crazy, and I was definitely a believer in abstinence – still am. Nonetheless, I beheld with my brown almond-shaped eyes the attention others girls received from the opposite sex. Where was mine? I didn't so much expect it from the White boys, but it was a little disheartening that even the brothas preferred vanilla beans. "Never mind all that," I'd tell myself. My Hershey bar was somewhere out there waiting for me. My hopes were strong as the sting of dark chocolate my buds yearned to taste.

In 2005 I entered the public education system. W.M. Gallatia High School quite savagely ripped the conservative scales from my eyes. I couldn't tell if I minded or not. I went from getting no attention to getting lots of attention. Not only was there a Black market, there was a White market, too, and I was in demand by the latter. Huh? I still don't understand what I could have possibly done to attract five White males. Up until this point, White males and Black females just didn't jive in my world. Still, while those offers were made available, I didn't care because that's not what I wanted.

New-age-Plaidville-Florida life just mocked me and jeered: "Too bad. Little do you know." All the Black boys raised with manners in a structured home that demanded nothing less than excellence were taken: by White girls. Or, so it seemed. Better stated, most of the intelligent Black boys who had good home training and appeared to be going somewhere in life chose White girls. What...a bigger school of fish with a true Black selection and the sistas are still getting jilted? This is when I began to get inexplicably angry.

~

Honestly, I'm 'bout to be real witchu. Straight up. My hide sears to ashes whenever I see a Black man with a White woman. Back in the day, I used to be okay with it. In fact, I was the one telling relatives "Oh it's just love. Let it go." We'd be watching an NFL game and someone would bust out with, "I don't want such-n-such team to win." I'd ask why and be rapidly greeted with, "'Cause the coach *(who was Black)* got a white wife." Originally, I thought this was a terrible attitude. I guess as it is with many things in life, I understand their view now that I'm older. Don't get me wrong. We aren't racist or anything. We have friends of many different cultures and ethnic backgrounds. Heck, I grew up in Plaidville which is, despite its diverse population, a predominantly White area. My best friend (who is no longer here with us, rest her soul) was white. All of that is great, but you know what? I can fathom the other side now.

Here's what you need to understand. It's not that Black men can't venture out and chart new territory. Go on. Be free. I, myself, have not closed the door to espousing other cultures though I prefer an African-American man. The problem comes when Black men say – and best believe many Black men do say – "I refuse to date a Black woman." What a slap in the face!

> *Now I want you to zero in right here and pay close attention. As the old folks say, "Hear me now, and hear me good." People have had a tendency to get this twisted. This is NOT the bashing of all African-American men. This is NOT a bitter Black woman. This is NOT by any means the hating of White women. This IS an African-American woman speaking for all African-American women who are hurt by the rejection they receive from the particular type of Black male being depicted here – the Black male who slams and bolts the door shut on women of his own race. Back to what I was saying…*

You said what? Excuse me, but who is your mother? Who is your father? Your sister? Your brother? What color are they? I said, WHAT COLOR ARE THEY? I just know you want to try saying that again. I just don't understand. I can't imagine how the mother of a Black son must feel to hear her child SHE raised speak those words.

This is what I want to know. What's wrong with me? Is it the hair? Not long enough? Not straight enough? Not light enough? Is it my skin? Not bright enough? What makes a White woman such a prize? I'm a prize, too. What makes you resent the thought of being with me, a girl of color? You're of color. Can you not see that you are in some way rejecting yourself? It can't be because I'm not smart. I'm in all the advanced courses. It can't be that I'm unrefined. I was raised amongst the finest of social settings. I'm well mannered. Just because your "better half" isn't Black, it doesn't mean that you've "arrived." I see it all the time. A Black man gets a little money then drops his chocolate honey for a vanilla kiss. Yep, they say it's not just a hankering for Whiteness, but I'm not about to believe that one for a split second. About every Black man I see in my city has a White woman. There is no way *all* of that is true love. You can't tell me that all those Black men so happened at the same time to fall in love with a White woman. Looks to me like they all went a'huntin' for a White woman. It's a fad, and it sickens me. Attention Black men: don't be a label ho. Buy Ralph Lauren because you genuinely like it – not because the tag says Ralph Lauren and everyone else is doing it.

Earth to reader. Do we still have a pulse? Get me the defibrillator! White chicks, this is not the time to get offended. I'm not saying that White women should not be prized. The question here is why Black women are not equally prized. Listen, AND open your eyes. I'm not the one you should be mad at here. In fact, you should be thanking me for blowing the cover on this particular type of Black man. Beware of him. Yes, they really do exist – the ones who are with you because of the color of your skin. Don't believe me? You need to remember I'm on the side of the fence you never get to be on. I and other Black females – their sisters, cousins, aunts, and mothers – get to hear what they say and see what they do when you aren't around. And what? You're mad because I called Black men dating White women a fad? Well what would you think if suddenly there was an unmistakably large number of Chinese men dating Indian women? Would you not at the very least find the spurt to be…interesting? It would not mean that none of it was true love, but would you not question the integrity of the love in a percentage of those relationships? Anyways, back to what I was saying…

In case you couldn't tell, I'm feeling rejected, and it don't taste no better with the passing of the days. What are Black girls supposed to do? Heck, what are White stags supposed to do? I don't know about my sistas, but I'm fixin' to cross over. I'm going to get me a white man and prance in front of every brotha I see. If this game is going be played it's not going to be a one person show. Yep, blink twice. That's me you see on the field looking fly in my stilettos and all. Best believe, two can play this game.

~

So, I figured if I couldn't get any love from the brothas I'd start taking up my other offers. My senior year of high school I dated my first White guy, Greg Collins. His hair and eyes were the color of brown autumn leaves. Compared to me, he looked as tall as a tree. The way we hitched is the way any hitching ought to go whether it's interracial or not – by chance. Originally, we weren't thinking twice about each other. He wasn't on the hunt for a Black girl, and despite the war I waged on Black guys, I was not trying to catch a White boy. We were friends and nothing more. We shared the same group of friends and the same table in our Honors English course.

When the homecoming dance was around the corner, I thought I'd just be going with my group of friends. That was good enough for me. A date was not on my radar when C.J., as he was better known, asked me to do him the honors. Even at this point I did not take any of this seriously. Everyone in our click was pairing off just for that one special night. It was no big deal until I was talking to one of the females in our group, Ayala Balasubramanian, about homecoming plans. At the end of our conversation she threw a curve ball that knocked the wind out of me.

"Ayvaunn, I have to tell you something."

"What?"

"C.J. likes you."

"…*(awkward silence)* Ok…"

"He plans to ask you to be his girlfriend later. He's really serious about it. I just wanted to give you the heads up."

I was absolutely speechless. Of the White guys in my pursuit, I sure as heck did not think he was one of them. To make matters worse, I'd have to go through homecoming with this secret of sorts burning inside of me. I wasn't supposed to know how he really felt about me, and darn it, I wasn't sure how I felt about him. Yeah, he was very smart. He was truly sweet. Being wealthy never hurt anyone. He even owned a dolphin. I'd never heard of anyone in our whereabouts who owned a dolphin, but that little fun fact was beside the point. There were just no *real* objections. Why not try something new? After all, the idea of giving genteel vanilla a try had always teased me. I had nothing to lose.

~

The homecoming dance was fast approaching, and the W.M. Gallatia Senior High School student body was a'buzz. Talk of clever homecoming t-shirt designs could be heard in the passing of student clusters on the hall as well as amongst my bio click in my 8:00 a.m. Advanced Placement Biology II class. Girls and boys alike bragged on their pre-party, dinner party, and after party plans. Yet, the biggest talk of all centered on who was taking who to the dance. When I shared that I was going with C.J., Brendan Hope, one of my Caucasian buddies, looked at me kind of stunned.

"Uh…Oh… Really?" he muttered in a voice strangely low for his robust vocals. I stared at him for a moment. He'd turned his head from me.

"Yeaaaah," I replied.

~

I'd stayed up all night on Friday getting beautiful for the dance to be held the following evening. My hair had to be perfect. My nails were dressed in jet black with a touch of silver glitter for shine. In the midst of last minute prepping on the night of the dance, my phone buzzed with a text.

"Hey." It was from Brendan. This was no surprise, because we chatted often. "'Sup?"

"Gettin ready 4 the dance."

"Wat u wearin?"

"A fitted black velvet floor length."

"Sounds hot."

"Ha. Thnx. Guess u'll c it 2nite."

"Not goin."

"Omg y not?!"

"I was gonna ask u 2 the dance."

I just about dropped the phone. How could he tell me a thing like this? Why would he tell me something like this? And right now? At that point in the game, I felt that was info he should have kept to himself. Ticked off, I don't think I responded after that. It was time to go spend the evening with C.J..

~

Sure as Ayala predicted, a few weeks after homecoming C.J. unleashed his little secret on me. It was true. He liked me. He wanted to date, and I acquiesced. To be totally truthful, no other guy I've entertained to this very day – vanilla or chocolate – has been able to fill his shoes. Never has anyone asked me "How are you?" and genuinely meant it. Never has anyone remembered things about me and my schedule that even I forget. Isn't it always the small things? He even put up with my giddy bubbly personality, craziness, and occasional outbursts of soul-sista spice. He respected my body. My vanilla experience was bliss.

There isn't too much to say about our relationship. We were two simple people who loved simple things. We were also two people dedicated to the world of academia which consumed much of our time. The mere fact of being in each other's presence, whether in person or through cyber space, was good enough for us. During three healthy intervals of our school day, we got to be close to each other physically – though not friskily. During our night-long chats every night online, we meshed mentally. The latter is most invaluable in a relationship.

The most major outing we had since the dance was the last home football game of the Gallatia Senior High Cougars. C.J. thought it was an absolute sin that I was a senior in high school and had not attended a single cougar football game. So, there we sat on those cold bleachers where he made his first move.

"Ayvaunn, let me ask you a question."

"Uh huh?"

"If you were a pirate…"

I hope to this very day that I didn't give him a crazy look when these initial words stumbled out of his mouth.

"…would you want your parrot on this shoulder, or this shoulder?" he asked while perching his hand on my shoulder nearest his chest then wrapping his arm around me to reach my other ball and socket. *Awe.*

Laughing internally at the cheesy cleverness of his little inquisition, I rolled my eyes to each of my shoulders. Then my pupils popped up to the right to meet his blushing, grinning face.

"The left shoulder," I replied giggling.

I simply couldn't resist something as cute as that. Looking back on the relationship as a whole, he cared about me so inexplicably much. I was caught up. I got to thinking, "Dang if this is what life is like on the other side, Thank you, brothas, for paying me no mind. Vanilla and I are doing just fine."

~

Now that I've tasted vanilla, I'll never be the same. It was interesting that my first dip was streaked with the lemon twist of Brendan. I certainly never would have thought I'd get caught between two White guys. I was doing good to venture out with one guy let alone deal with two at the same time. Brendan and I were just friends, and I made sure it stayed that way even though he was confident he could bring into fruition *his* plans.

Despite the glorious rendezvous with C.J., I let it die. Yes, I experienced the wonders of the other side, but vanilla just didn't quite hit the spot in my hankering for love. I was missing something, and I *could* put my finger on it. I needed a man with soul. Darn human nature for only tantalizing me with what it appeared at the moment I could not have. If there's nothing else you ever learn about a Black female, know this. She always gets what she wants. I can 'bout taste it, and I *will* have my chocolate.

Checkmate City, Florida – joined at the hip of and sharing the same population as Plaidville – has been my current dwelling place since 2008 and the couple social scene looks even bleaker. Many of the sistas are still flying solo. When I stand in a swarm of Black men with their White women, I still feel the sting. When I see that one Black couple, I can hardly contain my excitement. One day I'll find a brotha – my brotha – who believes a Black woman is a prize.

~

Seed of cacao, melt on my tongue
Leave me wide-eyed and drunken
I *still* cannot resist your delight
I *still* yearn for your boldness
Seize me by my senses
Tight

CONNECTING THE DOTS

Life was good in Miami, FL. My life as an only child had been writing itself on 2593 Leafy Palm Drive for fourteen years. My family moved there when I was three years of age. Our home was a nice two story brick edifice on the corner of a street just inside Sandy Beach, our community. Two broad wooden cream pillars bolstered a small awning above the front entry of our house. Just above the front door on the second story was a very large window in the shape of a *half* circle – perhaps an omen that never should have been overlooked in the purchasing of the home. Fond memories and not-so-fond memories rolled about the house all the way up until 2007 when not-so-fond memories started to look not-so-bad.

People always have a hard time believing our story – not only friends but, so hurtfully, family. Maybe that's why I tend to shy away from talking about it. While my family and I were in the heat of this threatening sequence of events, people thought we were crazy. Let me clarify. People thought my mother was crazy, but I assure you. She wasn't. It didn't help that my father, who also witnessed some of these events, was so nonchalant about our situation. Some people even dared to wonder aloud if he might be responsible. And me? I was just the child. Though at a point in this vicious game, I was so certainly accused by the police as being the cause of these freakish happenings. I wasn't. There were no answers as to why these people – yes, a group of people – were making repeated attempts to break into our home *while* we were home. There was no comprehendible reason as to how they could so easily evaporate upon the calling of the police and then could conjure their amorphous selves immediately following the police's departure. I suppose. I suppose blaming me was the effort of the authorities – just as perplexed as we – to make sense of the "benign" yet twisted reports from 2593 Leafy Palm Drive accumulating in their files. Of the variety of officers dispatched to our home, the majority of them did not believe us. It annoyed them that we were calling constantly. Well, that is after we got over the initial shock from these goosebump-raising occurrences. At first, we weren't calling. When you don't believe your eyes, when you're too busy rechecking your own sanity, sometimes calling the police slips your mind.

~

"I saw a pair of red eyes in my sleep," Mama confided in me. "It was so real, as if they were watching me."

Mama was greatly disturbed by this strange apparition. She's a short, brown-skinned, apple-shaped, woman. This condition of "shortness," I believe, causes all of her emotions to be highly concentrated. Simply describing Mama as cautious does not do her justice. I declare she must be half hawk. At the time, however, I did not know why this dream would unnerve Mama so much. Well, one thing did cross her mind for a split second - voodoo. Being a woman of Louisiana, she was aware of voodoo and black magic practiced in certain parts. In some areas of the Deep South people sweep their porch nightly to remove any possible traces of black magic that could have been dropped in malice. One of my great aunts in fact is earnestly believed to have been victimized by voodoo. Her boyfriend was out of town when this occurred. When he returned to find his girlfriend extremely ill, he lamented over having forgotten to tell her not to eat food from this particular woman. When my great aunt ate the ribs this strange woman prepared for her, she became vehemently ill and had to be hospitalized. She vomited profusely, defecated sizable white living organisms with many legs, lost her hair in full locks, and ultimately died. Mama had already tossed that fear aside before I spoke up. Having grown up in a Christian family, I ensured the dispelling of my mother's flitting fear by telling her "Wherever the Lord dwells, surely, the devil cannot." Physically, I sought to console my mother in her distress. Mentally, I did not take the matter seriously. After all, it was just a dream: a dream that was over and no longer had to be dealt with.

The other part of this story that bolsters the "unbelievable factor" is the extent to which intuition and dreams play a role. I had always found dreams to be confounding. The old folks ascertain dreams are far from nonsense: they mean something. Science claims another: dreams are merely a malleable compilation of thoughts one experiences – visible nothingness. Mama always said the elders knew. After surviving the life I lived four years ago, I know for a fact that Mama was right. The gray-haired were soundly seated on their rockers. The elders also spoke of "following your first mind" and being "led of the Spirit." That too is true. Sure as they said snow comes again if the downy lasts three days on the ground, Mama was right. The old folks knew.

~

"I got up around 3:00 a.m. last night, because I had to use the restroom," Mama shared with me one weekday morning. "As I was going down the hallway to the restroom, I noticed a red light on the wall. It was following me. To check myself, I took a few extra steps in various directions. The light still followed. I asked myself if it could be fireflies. That had to be the sleep talking, because that's a stretch I know doesn't make sense."

"Maybe it was just kids playing with a laser," I rationalized. Not the slightest clue could I summon as to what the strange red light might be, let alone why it would be following my mom.

"No, this was too big to be a laser like that." Mama formed her index finger and thumb to the guesstimated diameter. It certainly was larger than the pinpoint beam of a pocket laser. Words failed me. "Do weapons have beams on them?" she proceeded to inquire. I knew some did, but I did not want to scare my mom, for one. Secondly, I couldn't bring myself to believe something like that could happen. Nevertheless, Mama was waiting on an answer. With deep reluctance I muttered:

"Yes, some do."

My mom stared pensively. "I'm going to call a gun shop."

Sure enough after I returned from school that day Mama had dug up the answer to her question. "I called the gun shop, and yes, there are guns with lasers attached. To see for myself the size of the light, I dropped by the shop. Shelley, the light I saw on the wall last night is the same size of the lasers on the guns."

Once again, I was left speechless. What are you supposed to say after hearing something like that? My mom was obviously even more disturbed by this newfound discovery. Yet honestly, there was nothing we could do except pray. That we did. From that point forward, however, Mama could never really sleep again. She was deprived of sleep – unlike my father. Daddy was told of the strange incident, too, but that did not mean much. He is an easy going man. He was not concerned. He, like me, fished for some reasonable explanation and left it at that. For nights on end Mama would be up and about in the house at odd hours of morning. Attempts at sleep were pointless, for they yielded nothing more than sporadic intervals of teasing shut-eye.

~

"I think I was followed when I came to pick you up from school," my mom said in distress. Trees and buildings whizzed by as I gazed out the car window. Mama's words struck my eardrums, but they weren't quite resonating with me.

"For some reason, out of all the cars behind me, my attention was grabbed by this vehicle. I don't know why. When I looked in my rearview mirror it was not even close to me but far back. Other vehicles even got in between us, but when I got in the carpool line, this car pulled onto the lot after me but did not stop. It just kept on going around the parking lot full speed to the next parking lot exit. That's not normal. If you don't have a student to drop off, there's no need to pull onto the parking lot only to drive right back out going in the same direction. The person didn't even need to turn around. I find that suspicious. When you're on campus, I want you to be aware of your surroundings. You have to walk outside between classes to different buildings, so you don't need to be getting caught outdoors by yourself during passing hour."

I just kept gazing out the window. I never knew what to say to these things. I knew my mother had all her wits about her. At the same time I did not *want* to believe any of this strange stuff was happening. That was for the movies. Out of caution and respect I finally met my mother's words with a response.

"Yes ma'am."

From that point, I decided to trust Mama's judgment and instincts. I put forth more effort to be conscious of my surroundings.

~

"I had this dream that I was entering our house from the garage," Mama shared. "Everything was the exact layout of our house and so vivid. When I stepped out of the kitchen into the family room I saw the base of the stairs, and a man was descending the steps. As he did, I heard him say, 'I've been waiting for you.' I could only see him from the mid-chest down. He had on a pale yellow jacket. I don't know why I couldn't see his face. I wish I could have seen his face," she moaned.

~

It had been a long day at school, and Mama and I had just gotten home. I threw down my bag and hopped on the family room couch. It was time to chill before hitting the books. Mama joined me except she sat in the wing-back chair situated in front of the window facing the backyard. As we were watching one of my favorite TV shows:

"Did you see that?" The words sauntered haphazardly from my mother's limp mouth. Our television was positioned in a large entertainment center half of which had glass doors.

"What?"

My mother was silently observing something I was missing. Neither one of us moved. Apparently in the reflection of the entertainment center glass, Mama saw framed in the window behind her the silhouette of a tall slender man. He was staring at us lounging, and Mama was staring at his rigid frame in the reflection of the glass. It's probably safe to say that neither of them was *totally* sure of the other's awareness. The intruder was not sure if my mother was watching the TV or him, and my mom did not want to be sure that she was looking at a man in our backyard. She wanted to believe it was the new trees Daddy planted. Despite her wishes, when the tall body turned to the side and slowly eased away, a baseball cap appeared: a dead giveaway. Mama did not choose to reveal to me what she had seen until later that evening. For, it was only then that she convinced herself to accept what she could not deny to be true. No tree wears baseball caps. There had been a criminal in the backyard, and his identity was still hidden.

~

Strange, unidentifiable pieces of mail addressed to my father began to arrive at our home. These envelopes contained scrap paper with "Thought you might be interested in this" etched on it in unfamiliar hand writing. Also inside the envelopes were articles on life insurance for one's spouse. Another random article snip-it spoke about a certain "her" being in a car accident that she could not avoid. Once again, my father had nothing to say about these strange parcels. My mother's friends thought she was blowing the letters out of proportion. Then again, many of her friends began to blow her off when she would share with them the mysterious activities she was observing. It's sad. There have been many cases in the news where victims tried to cry out for help in the midst of their troubles but were ignored because of their outlandish testimonies. Their persistent stories were discounted as paranoia. For many of them, the shushing of their outcries by civilians and authorities alike resulted in their death. Yet as my family learned, even if the authorities believe your story there's no protection they can give you until your stalker actually enters your home or harms you. That said, people should still listen.

Because my mother would always be awake in the wee hours of the morning when our stalkers frequented our property, the enemy's plans were always thwarted. *It is a shame that a criminal has not broken the law until they break into or vandalize your home.* Whenever they were about to make their move, some sign of my mother's alert movements would be detected, and they would return to their vehicles parked at odd locations in the street network of our neighborhood. They came to realize that we, or my mother at least, were too smart and aware of their actions for them to be able to catch us in our home. Better stated, God divinely used my mother's insomnia as a deterrent to keep the enemy from breeching the security of our home. As a result, they moved their schemes to venues beyond our personal property. During this course of events, our stalkers had been studying our daily routine. They knew exactly when we would be where, the cars we drove, and who drove which vehicle. Whenever we'd turn into our neighborhood, there'd be an unmistakable toot of a car horn. Think what you want, but you know when there is and is not cause for someone to blow their horn. Nine times out of ten even if the incident does not involve you, you're aware of what might be the cause for such blowing. However, there was never any necessity, and the tooting, paired with a consistent flashing of the headlights, was enough for us to know it was a reference to us.

With each new piece added to this strange puzzle of our lives, my mother became increasingly aware. Don't even ask why my father never became more conscious. I simply don't know. Mama was always watching her rear view mirror. She came to recognize the new-common presence of certain vehicles. *They never stuck with just one vehicle.* Once again, there's nothing the police can do if someone is just following you. I'm telling you the enemy was smart, but they could not help but come to terms with the fact that God enabled Mama to be just as sharp as they were. She no longer counted anything as a small detail. Everything meant something. She began to read people's behavior and body language. This reading was often the dead giveaway when situations looked to be otherwise normal. It is this ability to analyze body language that people on the outside looking in lack. This is one of the most vital missing pieces that prevents them from taking our story seriously.

~

Buzz

That was my cue. I dropped my cell phone back into my bag, grabbed my things, and strolled out of the doors of my high school library. The click of my heels on the concrete echoed as I descended the sunbaked steps from the second story of the building. I was a little taller than usual that day. It took an infinitesimal moment longer for the view of Mama's red Mazda in the near-distant lot to slip away from my view. Every few clicks, I swerved my head over each shoulder and let my eyes survey the empty campus. One or two stragglers who were supposed to be in class roamed here and there. Lucky for me, I had senior early release. I didn't have to fight the parking lot rush because student dismissal was not for another two hours. Mama's car hastened back into my view as I turned the curve of the sidewalk, but that day she was standing outside of the car. She was motioning anxiously for me to go in a building. Immediately, I veered into the building at my right. As I stood inside the glass doors, I tried to call my mom – multiple times. No answer. My heart began to race. My pulse was pounding in my ears. The muffled voices of teachers lecturing weaseled their way into my increasingly aimless thoughts. Mere minutes stretched ad infinitum. Then she rushed into the building. *Exhale.*

"You're coming out of this school!" Mama exclaimed. "When I was pulling into the parking lot, I checked to make sure no one drove in behind me. No one did. In the split-second it took me to pull up to the curb and call you to come out, two men were pulled up behind me. They had to have been waiting for me on the parking lot. *During this time, Mama was on an extended sub assignment at a school just down the street from my school. Hence, our routine for that month was very consistent. Around 2:45 p.m. Mama would drive five minutes down the road to come pick me up from school, and every day I exited from the same building.* Out of the years you've been here, I've never seen those men before. They weren't dropping anyone off, or picking anyone up. Out of the five buildings on campus, they were watching the building you were supposed to come out of. Then they noticed me noticing them. They got really fidgety. The man in the passenger seat began to slide down in his seat and hide his face. The driver got on his cell phone and began reaching for something below. I desperately tried to get you to answer your phone so that you'd stay in the library, but you never answered. I couldn't have you come to the car. I was frantically watching for you to come out of the building. Not knowing what else to do, I just got out of the car and began walking towards my trunk with my phone flipped open. I was trying to sneak a picture of their license plate, but there was no way for them to know that. For all they knew, I was just dialing a number while headed to my trunk. All of a sudden the car behind me shot backwards, without the driver even looking behind, and just sped off. Thank God you didn't question me when I told you to go into a building. Shelley, I whole heartedly believe they were going to kidnap you. There was no reason for them to have that kind of reaction to me. Any other people would not have been paying me any mind. They would not have gotten nervous because I was paying attention to them. What kind of grown man slides down in his seat trying to hide just because a woman – a total stranger – is looking at him? Most of all, there is absolutely no reason to speed away so suddenly just because I got out of my car and began walking toward the trunk of my own car. They just did not want me to be able to identify them. They had no other business on that parking lot. If they wanted me, I was outside of my car and vulnerable. They could have done whatever they wanted to do to me. They were waiting for you."

That was the Friday before spring break. From that day I never returned to B.E. Wallace Senior High School or – for many years – that area of Miami again.

~

There are a countless number of other eerie situations that plagued our lives. Here, I've touched on the apexes of the beginning, middle, and end. All of this spanned over a course of about two years. I'd love to be able to say that there's no possible way I'd ever be able to tell you everything, but I can't say that. The truth is I'm afraid. I'm afraid that even if I attempted to reveal to you all of the dots you would not be able to connect them, and yet again I'd just be made out to be "not all there."

All through elementary school they want to teach you about pattern recognition. Assignment instructions read something like "Examine the following sequence of figures. Draw the figure you think should appear next." As we progress to higher levels of education, we're asked to fulfill the same task. The problems just get increasingly convoluted. We all master at least the elementary recognition of patterns. That elementary recognition, plus the gut feeling of human nature, is all you need to know. That's all you need to be able to connect the dots that form that roughly clear picture that something is amiss. To know that someone is slyly trying to break into your home. To know that someone is following you. To know that this enemy has a complicated yet brilliant system that dishearteningly allows them to never get caught. To know that you and your enemy are the only ones who *know*. To know they are somewhere mocking your misery because NO ONE believes you, sometimes not even you. To know all too well that you aren't crazy. To know that you see what you see. You hear what you hear. Though ever so slight, you notice what you notice. You're connecting the dots. You're following the sequence of figures. It all adds up, and your instinctive gut sickeningly but unmistakably confirms. You know without a doubt what the next figure is, and you refuse. You refuse to draw it because you know that it is the embodiment of your ultimate demise. All at the same time, you know your enemy is morbidly, happily drawing it for you. You must stop them. BUT. You. Can't. Stop. Them.

ABOUT THE AUTHOR

Words live vicariously through her – her being Ayvaunn Penn. The recipient of two honorary scholar awards and praised by faculty as the pride of her college's English department, this young writer and actress is determined to change the world through the art of words and storytelling. Not only does she love being the teller of the tales, she has an equal love for using her body as the medium through which stories come alive.

Her passion does not stop there, however. Merging her gift of writing with her love for African-American culture and heritage, she is currently a senior editor for one of the leading black news platforms with nearly half a million subscribers nationwide. Ms. Penn has been a part of this organization since the spring of 2011. It was in that same year that she founded *Your Black Poets* – currently the number one black poetry website. Miss Penn also writes daily Bible devotionals to which you can obtain an email subscription by visiting www.ayvaunnpenn.wordpress.com.